WHAT FAMOUS INVENTORS ARE SAYING ABOUT THIS BOOK

NETWORK C. PRIMETYME

Inventor of the
TV Commercial

"This book gives
new meaning to
the expression
'HARD SELL' "!

**OILDRECK
BEN OPEC**

Inventor of
Energy Conservation

"Nothing runs out
of gas faster
than this book!"

MORE

DOW P. KEMIKAL

Inventor of the Outdoor Barbecue

"I've seen better things than this at book burnings!"

NIXXON M. FROSTMONEY

Inventor of the Big Alibi

"There is absolutely no excuse for this book!"

Get With The Experts And Get This Book So You Can Enjoy The Exquisite Pleasure Of Knocking It Along With Them...

AL JAFFEE'S

MAD

INVENTIONS

Written and Illustrated by
AL JAFFEE
Edited by
ALBERT B. FELDSTEIN

WARNER BOOKS

A Warner Communications Company

WARNER BOOKS EDITION

*Copyright © 1978 by Al Jaffee
and E.C. Publications, Inc.*

All rights reserved.
No part of this book may be reproduced without permission.
For information address E.C. Publications, Inc., 485 Madison
Ave., New York, N.Y. 10022

ISBN 0-446-86116-2

Title **"MAD"** used with permission of its owner,
E.C. Publications, Inc.

*This Warner Books Edition is published by
arrangement with E.C. Publications, Inc.*

Warner Books, Inc.,
75 Rockefeller Plaza, New York, N.Y. 10019

Ⓦ A Warner Communications Company

Printed in the United States of America

Not associated with Warner Press, Inc. of Anderson, Indiana

First Printing: March, 1978

10 9 8 7 6 5 4 3 2 1

FOREWORD

Al Jaffee is an inventor. In addition to the gadgets, gimmicks, and other glitch that you'll find in the following pages, for instance,

   a chapter whose only virtue is that
   it signals the end of this book. And
   so you'll find that Jaffee will help
   YOU become as creative and
   inventive as he is, which is exactly
   what he's done for me. For how else
   could I have written a FOREWORD
   in the measly two pages he allotted
   for the CONTENTS?

nick meglin

NICK MEGLIN
Associate Editor
MAD Magazine

Chapter One

We've all heard the expression, "Ahead of its time". Well, throughout history inventors have suffered bitter disappointment because their ideas were ahead of their time and thus were rejected by the public. With this in mind, we checked back into history. Lo and behold, we came up with a treasure trove of inventions that were flops in their own time, but went on to be re-invented at a later date with huge success.

INVENTIONS THAT DIDN'T MAKE IT IN THEIR OWN TIME

INVENTION: The Typewriter
INVENTOR: Underwood Fingerpeck
DATE: June 24, 1748

A special keyboard is connected by rods to hammers with alphabet letters on them. When a key is struck its inked letter is pounded down onto paper. Correspondence is thus made neat and legible.

8

REASON FOR FAILURE: Impossible to find a secretary who could type more than 60 words a week.

INVENTION: Hair Blower
INVENTOR Feodor Follicle
DATE: August 5, 1679

DESCRIPTION: Flexible hose is connected to large bellows. User jumps up and down on bellows while holding hose to hair for drying.

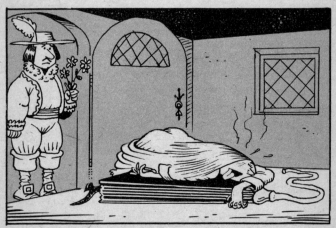

REASON FOR FAILURE: User was always too tired to go out after all this exercise.

INVENTION: Power Mower
INVENTOR: Humus J. Crabbegrasee
DATE: December 3, 1841

DESCRIPTION: Squirrel cages are mounted on either side of circular blade. When squirrels run, blades spin and cut grass.

REASON FOR FAILURE: Squirrels ran the wrong way and cut inventor to shreds.

INVENTION: Television
INVENTOR: Thomas P. Vakumtoob
DATE: May 18, 1897

DESCRIPTION: A series of glass prisms are precisely located throughout town. When a performer appears in front of the master prism, his image is simultaneously "transmitted" to a number of "receiving" prisms.

REASON FOR FAILURE: Lousy performance.

INVENTION: Automatic Shaver
INVENTOR: Beardsly Kleenface
DATE: November 23, 1869

DESCRIPTION: Plunger type instrument causes rapid spinning of razor blades.

REASON FOR FAILURE: Wives borrowing device to peel potatoes dulled the blades.

INVENTION: The Wig
INVENTOR: Ngg Bkingb
DATE: 2,464,531 B.C.

DESCRIPTION: Mammoth hair arranged in such a manner as to fit over a human head as a cover for baldness.

REASON FOR FAILURE: Every square inch of everyone's body at this time was covered with hair.

INVENTION: Airplane
INVENTOR: Zigmund Dimwicz
DATE: February 29, 1714

DESCRIPTION: Two long bars are attached to the sides of a chair's back. Six large birds are attached to each bar. A loud shout of "Aloft, ye foul birds!" sets their wings flapping.

REASON FOR FAILURE: Birds migrated to Aukland Islands taking inventor and invention with them and never returned.

INVENTION: The Swiss Army Knife
INVENTOR: Heidi Heidiho
DATE: April 1, 1515

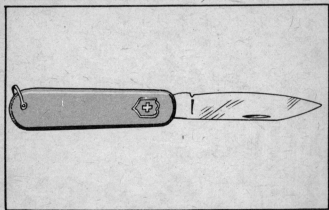

DESCRIPTION: The main attraction of this invention is that the blade folds out of the way and looks harmless to the enemy. In battle, however, blade can be quickly unfolded for attack.

REASON FOR FAILURE: During attack, blade had a tendency to fold and cut off Swiss army man's hands.

INVENTION: Flashlight
INVENTOR: Eveready Drycell
DATE: March 21, 1821

DESCRIPTION: A tube-like affair is filled with female fireflies. One end is capped with magnifying glass, and the other with a large cork. When pointed at a dark spot, it gives illumination.

REASON FOR FAILURE: During the firefly mating season, the inventor was swarmed and suffocated to death by male fireflies.

INVENTION: The Elevator
INVENTOR: Fortney Lift
DATE: April 25, 1401

DESCRIPTION: Elevator gondola is attached to hot air balloon. As heat increases, balloon rises.

REASON FOR FAILURE: Most towns only had one story buildings.

INVENTION: The Vacuum Cleaner
INVENTOR: Hoover Sukks
DATE: October 17, 1897

DESCRIPTION: Flexible hose is attached to pogo-stick like device. Up and down pumping creates vacuum. User thus hops around cleaning carpet.

REASON FOR FAILURE: Complaining downstairs neighbors.

INVENTION: The Skateboard
INVENTOR: Oswald Skinskab
DATE: November 11, 1819

DESCRIPTION: Four wheels sawed from a round log are affixed to a board. Rider simply goes down road and steers by leaning body to right or left.

REASON FOR FAILURE: No paved roads.

INVENTION: Power Boat
INVENTOR: Hans Fingerdike
DATE: May 6, 1601

DESCRIPTION: A windmill, located at the rear of a boat, is connected to a propeller below the waterline. The turning windmill blades turn propeller which pushes boat forward.

REASON FOR FAILURE: Low bridges.

INVENTION: Eyeglasses
INVENTOR: Uggly Bleindbat
DATE: 3245 B.C.

DESCRIPTION: Two convex or concave shaped pieces of ice are held together with yak bone and thong and suspended over the eyes.

REASON FOR FAILURE: They melted when the Ice Age came to an end.

INVENTION: Flush Toilet
INVENTOR: Tayka Dumpp
DATE: July 19, 1642

DESCRIPTION: Ceramic bowl is located over hole in floor. Flushing is accomplished when special arm lowers bucket into nearby well or stream and pours water down chute into bowl.

REASON FOR FAILURE: Having to move house too frequently when basement became full.

INVENTION: Smoke Detector
INVENTOR: Richard A. Jaffee
DATE: October 1, 1947

DESCRIPTION: Funnels over houses are connected to pipes that lead to fire station. Excessive smoke from a fire comes into fire house. Firefighters quickly note address on pipe and race off to do their duty.

| 300 EAST 59 ST. | 12 DUNCAN AVE. | | 155 PEBBLE LANE | 400 EAST 56 ST. | 77 7TH AVE. |

REASON FOR FAILURE: Smoke from first emergency filled fire house and asphixiated firemen.

INVENTION: Electric Guitar
INVENTOR: Django Catgut
DATE: August 11, 1908

DESCRIPTION: A large kite connected to a fine, insulated wire is sent aloft during an electrical storm. Current from lightning flows into guitar, permitting much louder sounds.

REASON FOR FAILURE: An unprecedented spell of good weather.

INVENTION: Washing Machine
INVENTOR: R. Maytag Whirlpoole
DATE: February 3, 1901

DESCRIPTION: Clothes are placed in steel gripper "hands". Crank causes scrubbing action on scrubbing board until clothes are clean.

REASON FOR FAILURE: Steel gripper "hands" wore out too often, necessitating a return to wife's hand scrubbing.

Chapter Two

The energy shortage, which is already critical, is going to get much worse as we've noted in another article in this book (Living in smaller spaces . . .). But there are many ways we can fight this battle of energy and money conservation. Here are some simple inventions for

CUTTING DOWN THE HIGH COST OF ENERGY

PEDALING FOR ENERGY

People spend a lot of time just sitting at home, in offices, in schools etc. Most of this time, either their hands, their feet or both are doing absolutely nothing. Here's how these worthy appendages can be turned into useful energy producers while at the same time providing healthful exercise for flabby citizens.

THE BICYCLE TYPE HAND OPERATED ENERGY GENERATOR

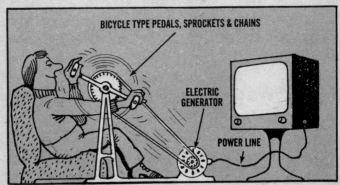

While watching TV hands or feet are utilized to produce energy required to operate the set.

THE WALKING, RUNNING AND JOGGING ENERGY GENERATOR

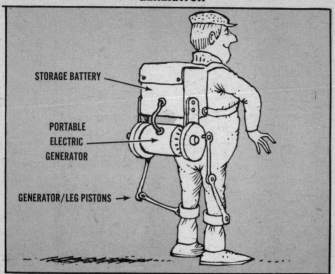

STORAGE BATTERY

PORTABLE ELECTRIC GENERATOR

GENERATOR/LEG PISTONS

This is basically an energy storage system. Pistons connected to wearer's legs generate power which is pumped into backpack storage battery for later use.

WALKING   **RUNNING**   **JOGGING**

THE LARGE CROWD TREADLE TYPE ENERGY GENERATOR

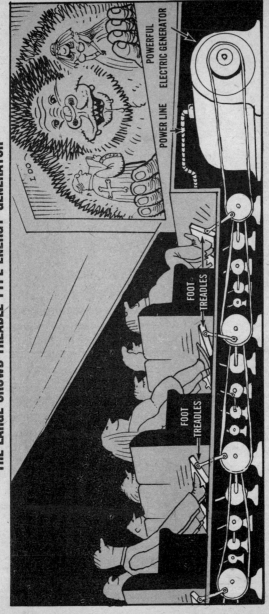

Watching movies, patrons use toy automobile type push-pedals which provide energy to operate projector, pop-corn machine and bathroom hand driers. System can also be effective in schools, stadiums, massage parlors and other places with large crowds.

THE SEE SAW FOOT POWERED ENERGY GENERATOR

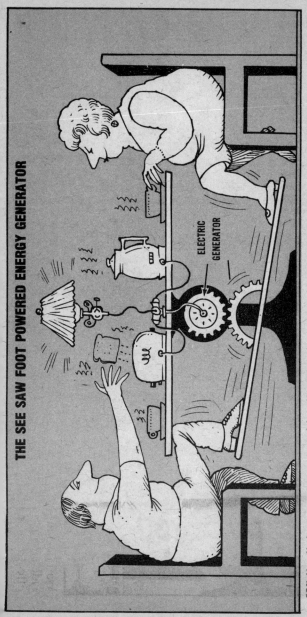

ELECTRIC GENERATOR

While dining, any number of family members can use this handy foot operated energy producer.

THE BUSY SIDEWALK ENERGY GENERATOR

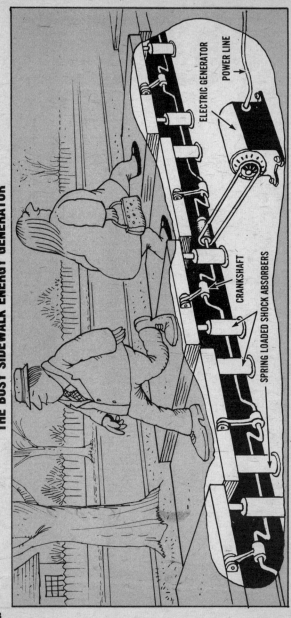

Many businesses and homes are located in busy areas with a lot of foot traffic. These feet act like machine pistons to power this sidewalk generator.

THE PET POWER SYSTEM OF ENERGY GENERATION

Our nation has millions of dogs who need daily exercise. The simple backyard device shown here provides this vital exercise while at the same time satisfying owner's energy needs.

ELECTRIC GENERATOR

Millions of miles are traveled by shopping carts daily. The device shown here makes each cart its own little electric plant to light up area where shopper is looking. This eliminates need for typically overbright, wasteful supermarket lighting.

Chapter Three

Years ago, when it came to flowers, the world was split into two main groups. Those who thought they were worth all the work and bother they required, and those who didn't. Then along came the miracle of science and this rift was healed. The miracle was *plastic flowers*. All the work and bother were eliminated. There may no longer be a split in the flower world, but the rest of the world is split worse than ever. So, with the flower solution in mind, here's how we can heal every other rift with . . .

A TROUBLE-FREE PLASTIC WORLD

PLASTIC PLANTS ARE SUPERIOR TO REAL ONES

REAL PLANTS

Real plants are a nuisance because they need constant care, die, get bugs and bloom whenever *they* feel like it.

PLASTIC PLANTS

Plastic plants need no care, come in every exotic variety, don't stink up the place and bloom all the time.

So far we've dealt with what seems like practical things for the plastic takeover. But now let's go into an area where a little more imagination is required. And remember, when plastic plants first came out there were scoffers who said "It'll never replace the real thing". So don't be a reactionary creep when you read about the wonders we project in a plastic world.

Having real children is a gamble. Parents never know what they'll (yecch!) get.

Real children are costly to raise. They consume food, clothing, and other expensive things.

Real children misbehave and often humiliate parents in front of company.

PLASTIC CHILDREN

Plastic children are no gamble. They are purchased according to age, sex, race, color, creed, etc.

Plastic children consume nothing. They can be placed in an attitude of quiet play to brighten the room.

Plastic children are neat and quiet before company. To add realism, they can be replaced yearly for older models to give "growing up" feeling.

REAL GUESTS

Some people have only boring friends. When they invite these clods to parties the yawning becomes deafening. If it's a special occasion, like trying to impress the boss and his wife, the hosts can count on their stupid, low-class friends to behave horribly.

PLASTIC GUESTS

Plastic guests (inexpensively rented) provide glamour without headaches. The room is filled with interesting conversation from all high class walks of life. They don't eat, drink or smoke which cuts down on expense and clean up. From time to time, "guests" can be moved around to lend realism. Also, photos sent to local newspaper society columns are very impressive.

REAL BUSINESS ASSOCIATES

Real business associates serve one function — they give a firm that big, important look. But they also give a firm that big, costly problem of high salaries.

PLASTIC BUSINESS ASSOCIATES

Plastic business associates can give a firm an even bigger look for less money. The Board of Directors shown here gets out as much work as the Board shown at the top of the page and yet the only live person is the stockholder standing in the doorway.

Real pets can cause property damage. Cat shown here scratching expensive upholstery.

Real pets have personal habits which masters must conform to or face disastrous consequences.

Real pets require special services. Shown here is lady cleaning canary cage. To show gratitude, bird has sung two songs in six years.

PLASTIC PETS

Plastic pets are trouble free. They don't scratch, bite, eat or —*ahem*— do anything else distasteful.

Plastic pets make no demands. A plastic dog will sit and be petted for hours without getting restless.

Plastic pets need no servicing. Cage shown here has built in tape of canary songs which can be played anytime.

REAL HUSBANDS AND WIVES

Anyone who knows anything about real husbands and wives knows what a revolting mess that can be. Any resemblance to romantic Hollywood notions is purely ridiculous. Which is why the divorce rate threatens to surpass the marriage rate.

PLASTIC HUSBANDS AND WIVES

Plastic husbands and wives can make marriages work. Life-like plastic figures are beautiful to look at and feel good from head to toe. No more squabbles, hair curlers, bad breath, and complaints. No more divorce. A yearly trade-in, like with a car, is all that's needed.

Chapter Four

Sooner or later each and every one of us is bound to be put upon by some careless slobs. Invited or not, they arrive in our homes and carelessly ruin the things we value. The following are inventions that take care of this problem.

HEALTH AND POSSESSIONS PROTECTORS

Some clods go visiting anywhere no matter how sick and germ laden they are. These pleasant looking, fashion coordinated masks protect you and your family without hurting visitor's feelings.

CHEERFUL, EASY TO ATTACH FACE MASK

TELEPHONE STERILIZER

Anyone who has used a phone after some garlic eater used it knows this problem. Automatic device hygienically deodorizes and disinfects.

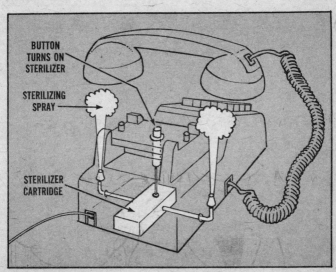

BUTTON TURNS ON STERILIZER

STERILIZING SPRAY

STERILIZER CARTRIDGE

BODY DOILIES

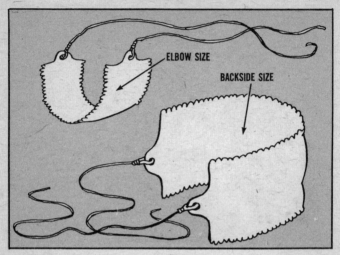

A good many people don't realize into what they've put their elbows and backsides before visiting you. These easy to wear doilies protect your furniture and upholstery.

Visitors are often carried away by the beauty of
your art objects and can't resist fondling and soiling
them. The electrified field created by this device is
an effective discourager.

MAGNETIC GLASS COASTER

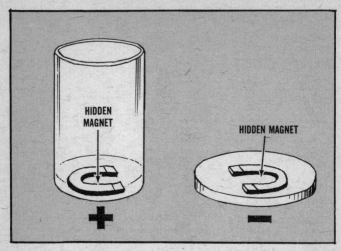

No matter how much you follow a sloppy guest around trying to put a coaster under his glass, he'll somehow miss it. The powerful magnets in the bottom of these glasses and coasters guarantee your table's safety.

ASH CATCHERS

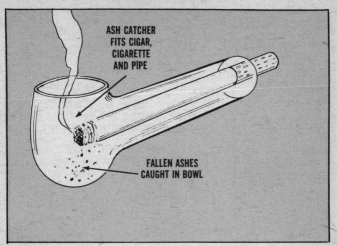

ASH CATCHER
FITS CIGAR,
CIGARETTE
AND PIPE

FALLEN ASHES
CAUGHT IN BOWL

Visitors who smoke can become thoughtless about dropping ashes. These cute, easy to use holders fit cigaret, cigar, and pipe, and stop this problem. Afterwards, a simple rinsing gets them ready for future use.

SPILL PROOF GLASSES

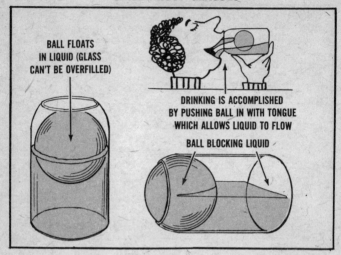

BALL FLOATS
IN LIQUID (GLASS
CAN'T BE OVERFILLED)

DRINKING IS ACCOMPLISHED
BY PUSHING BALL IN WITH TONGUE
WHICH ALLOWS LIQUID TO FLOW

BALL BLOCKING LIQUID

The worst, most destructive visiting slob problem is with drinkers. After a few blasts they start reeling around your living room spilling and splashing. These glasses take care of that nightmare.

BEMUSED HOSTESS

FUN-LOVING, DRUNKEN GUEST

AUTOMATIC TOILET DEODORIZER

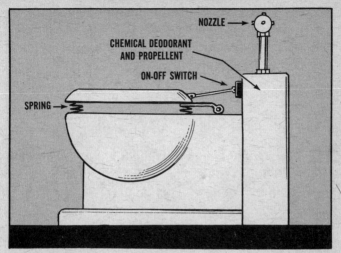

NOZZLE

CHEMICAL DEODORANT AND PROPELLENT

ON-OFF SWITCH

SPRING

In the interest of good taste we are not going to go into detail about *this* slob problem. The pressure switch in this toilet seat is activated when user rises setting off powerful deodorizing spray.

INDIVIDUAL TOOTHBRUSH HOLDER

Visitors using your bathroom may carelessly despoil exposed toothbrushes. That's not possible with this individual combination lock toothbrush holder rack.

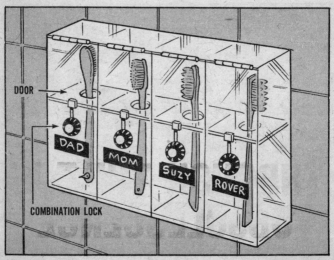

Chapter Five

Profit is what makes the world go round. And it doesn't take a genius to figure out there's no profit in making things that last forever. Just ask any maker of automobiles or large appliances. Things that break down are good for all of us. They keep the economy humming. Workers get paid to make replacements, manufacturers and stores profit from selling, and stockholders happily clip coupons. Of course, consumers and their bleeding heart lobbyists aren't too happy about this. But Yankee ingenuity comes to the rescue here. By cleverly building in a hidden breakdown point, manufacturers fool consumers who believe it's all happening through normal wear and tear. But there are still a lot of areas of manufacture where this sound principle is being ignored. These must be brought into line for the good of our nation, the capitalist system and the rather shaky premise of this article. So here is . . .

THE ROAD TO PROSPERITY THROUGH BUILT-IN OBSOLESCENCE

ELECTRIC OUTLET PRONG BENDER

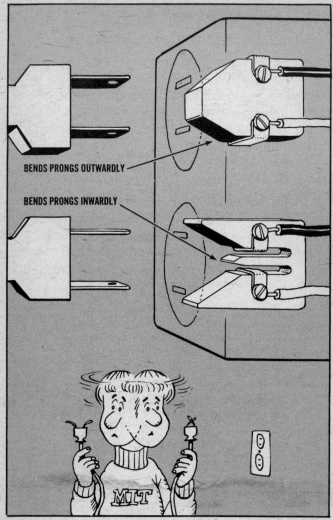

BENDS PRONGS OUTWARDLY

BENDS PRONGS INWARDLY

Plastic guides inside receptacle take prongs on different routes each time. After some back and forth bending, prongs snap off.

TANGLED TISSUES

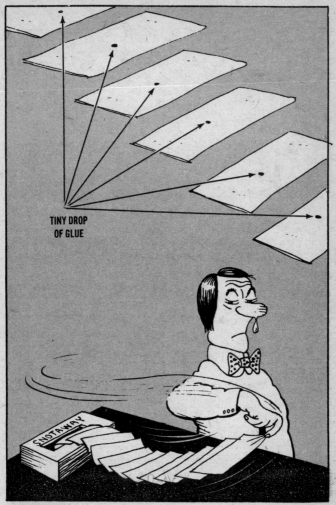

TINY DROP
OF GLUE

When packed, packing machine deposits tiny drop of glue every now and then on tissues. This causes several tissues to come out at same time. Box is used up fast.

ENVELOPE WITH FOUL
TASTING GLUE

When buyer of pack of envelopes tests taste of glue it is delicious. But one envelope in middle of pack has disgustingly foul-tasting glue that makes user almost throw-up. Rest of envelopes are usually discarded.

EXTENSION CORD FRAYER

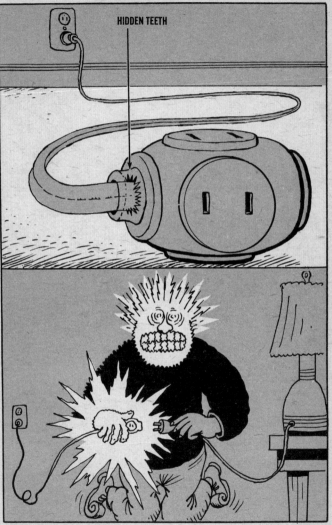

Tiny, invisible teeth cut slowly into cord every time it's moved until it finally breaks. User thinks it's from normal use.

SOFT LEAD SCREW HEAD

Soft lead embedded in screw heads cause screws to become useless. User blames rotten screwdriver.

BRISTLE CUTTING BRUSH

RAZOR SHARP CUTTING EDGES

Metal brush holders into which bristles are clamped are razor sharp and cut bristles during back and forth painting strokes.

BENDING TOOTHBRUSH BRISTLES

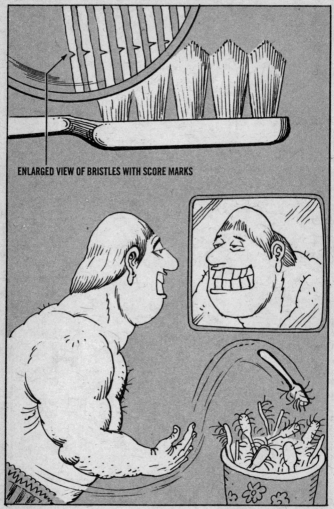

ENLARGED VIEW OF BRISTLES WITH SCORE MARKS

Each bristle is microscopically cut halfway through so it bends. User proudly thinks his vigorous brushing did it.

WATCH BAND ROT SPOT

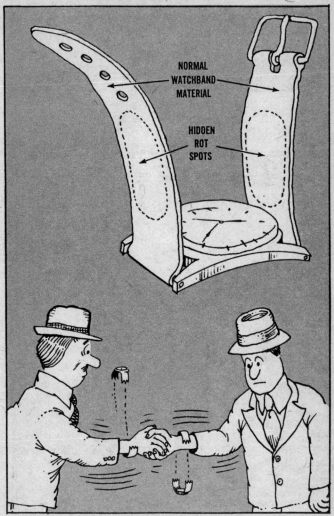

A special moisture collecting area designed into loop of strap, traps sweat and slowly rots band. Leather goes quickly. Metal takes a little longer.

Chemically treated paint contains highly active evaporating agent which makes it disappear right out of can. User thinks he used it up by putting on too thick a coat.

INSECT SPRAY ATTRACTANT

Clever chemical in spray kills insects on contact and impresses user. But poison chemical evaporates and leaves a residue of harmless *insect attracting* chemical. Place becomes infested and prompts user to spray again. Cycle keeps repeating endlessly.

DISAPPEARING STAMP GLUE

Postage stamps have glue that works fine when affixed to letter. But after a short while glue dries out
and turns to dust causing stamp to fall off. Letter is
returned and another stamp has to be purchased.

Chapter Six

THE SWISS ARMY KNIFE

REGULAR SWISS ARMY KNIFE

The regular Swiss Army Knife is terrific for Boy Scouts, but its military value is dubious.

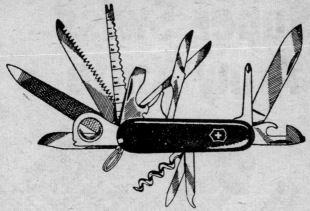

SWISS NAVY KNIFE*

If the Swiss Army Knife seems rather useless, it is nothing compared to the Swiss *Navy* Knife* as this clearly shows.

*Switzerland does not have a navy

Now for the *All New Super Swiss Knife.* ➤

The All New Super Swiss Army Knife

Some of you may have wondered why the Swiss Army Knife contains nothing but peaceful, Boy Scout-like items such as toothpicks, scissors, darning needles, etc. Well, that's because Switzerland has never gone to war, dummy. For a real *he-man's* army knife, turn the page.

He-man American Army Knife

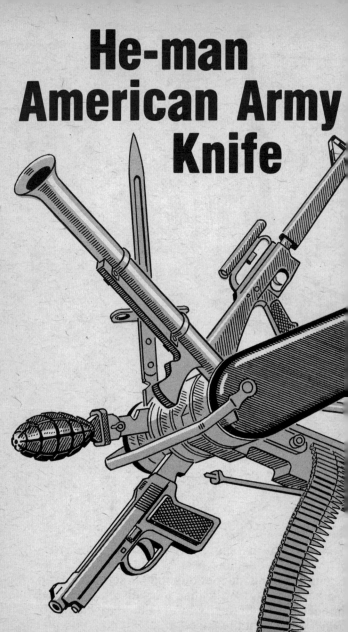

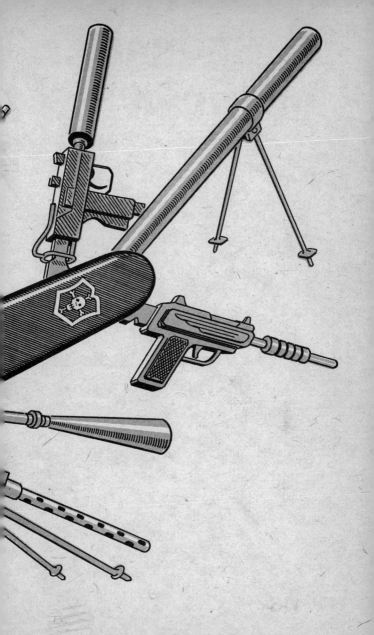

Chapter Seven

Sleep problems are major issues in our country. Sleeping workers not only waste time, but they are also dangerous to themselves and others. Anyone who has fallen asleep at a car wheel, or while operating a buzz saw will know what we're talking about. But the real problem isn't sleep. It's the *lack* of it. For if the people we just mentioned got a good night's sleep, they wouldn't be dozing off on the road, on the job, etc. And most of the people in this category are not carousers who stay up drinking, dancing and otherwise carrying on all night. No, they are mostly just everyday folk like you and me who toss and turn in bed all night only to fall asleep just before the alarm rings. So no wonder they have to sleep during the day. Now in order to help these poor, long-suffering insomniacs, here is something guaranteed to put anyone to sleep. (No, we don't mean this article, dummy!)

SURE-FIRE SLEEP AIDS

SLEEP INDUCING RECORDINGS

There are numerous recordings on the market today that are excellent for putting people to sleep. There are also those specifically made for that purpose. But not all people respond to the same sleep inducing sounds. Therefore, a variety is available and the list below should contain something for everyone.

*The soothing voice of a tax accountant explaining a 1040 form.

*The voice of Truman Capote reading the first three chapters of this book aloud.

*Old State of the Union speeches.

*New State of the Union speeches.

*The sound of snoring in the balcony of the U.S. House of Representatives.

"ROCKABYE BABY" BED DEVICES

One of the best sleep producers was that relaxed, secure feeling in infancy when our mothers rocked us to sleep. These devices recreate that feeling in the various ways shown.

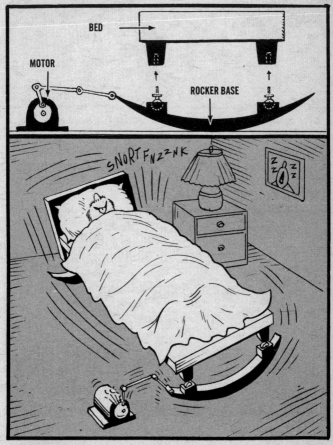

1 Rockers can be attached to any bed. Simple motor and arm connection then rocks bed at any set rate. Pleasant childhood memory soon induces sleep.

2   Gentle swaying of a boat does it for some people.
These easily attached springs are extremely sen-
sitive to the slightest motion and cause bed to
move exactly like a bobbing boat. People prone
to sea sickness should use caution — especially
when sleeping with others.

3   This set-up recreates the hammock effect which
is tremendously effective for many people who
instantly fall asleep in one on a lazy summer
afternoon. Candles that give off chemical smells
of fresh mown grass and recordings of buzzing
insects can be added for more realism.

4 This rocking effect is an idea borrowed from an ancient toy. A single, very heavy ball-like leg supports the bed. When tosser and turner goes into his restless act, bed sways in all directions and soon soothes user into blissful slumber.

OTHER SLEEP-INDUCING GIMMICKS AND DEVICES

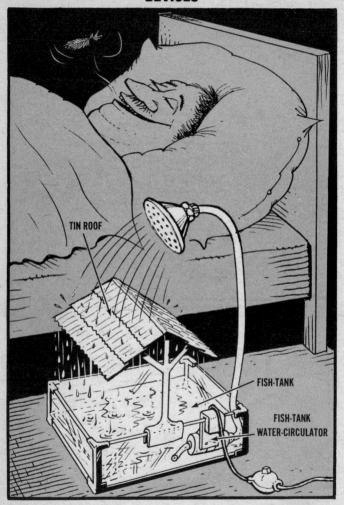

TIN ROOF

FISH-TANK

FISH-TANK
WATER-CIRCULATOR

1 Rain Sound. The gentle sound of rain on a tin roof is extremely soothing to many people. This device does it without creating anxieties about waking up to a lousy, dreary, rainy morning.

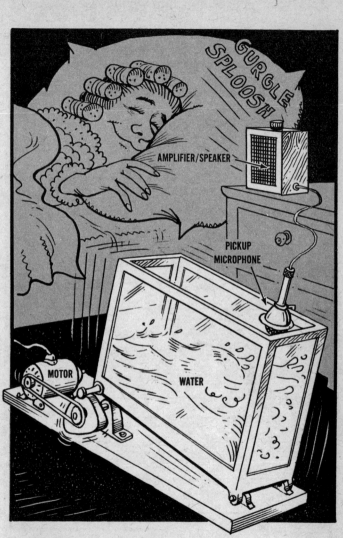

2 Pounding Surf. This turns many into instant sleepers. It recalls the pleasant, relaxed feeling of falling asleep at the beach. A sunlamp can be added for extra effect.

3 TV Tape Decks. For those who have this latest electronic home entertainment item the following material can work wonders. It consists of a series of taped TV shows that are guaranteed to put anyone to sleep when played back on your home TV player.

SURROUND WALLPAPER

Soothing wallpaper applied to ceiling and walls surrounds you with sleep inducing feelings. Pictured above is one type. Shown below are just a few of the many other soothing patterns available.

SHEEP COUNTER

Many older non-sleepers may still be partial to the old-fashioned "sheep counting" method of falling asleep. This device modernizes that procedure with monotonous moving pictures and hypnotic digital counter.

Chapter Eight

Anyone who has lived in a big city knows what hassles are from A to Z. This chapter is devoted to inventions that can help city dwellers live years beyond their normal 32 year life expectancy. It is divided into the three main hassles of city life. How to handle crime. How to handle parking. And how to handle doggie-do. So if you're one of the poor city slobs we're talking about, here are some ways to fight the system with our . . .

BIG CITY
SURVIVAL
KIT

GLITCH!

Section 1. Crime Problems

Big cities are full of criminals whom ordinary citizens feel powerless to fight. And then there are the criminals who are *not* politicians, policemen, and landlords. They are burglars and muggers. The ordinary citizen feels helpless against them too. But now to the rescue come the following devices.

LOADED HAT

This device is particularly effective in neighborhoods with a high incidence of hitting on the head. A sharp blow on plunger (A) explodes powder (B) and blasts tear gas into eyes of attacker. Resulting blindness, sneezing and crying effectively neutralizes him.

HOT HAND HANDBAG

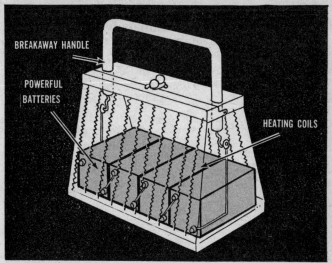

Bag is completely wired with heating coils. Powerful batteries are concealed in its bottom. When bag is grabbed, handle breaks away causing short circuit. Bag instantly reaches 300 degrees Fahrenheit, searing flesh off miscreant's hands.

BELLYWHOPPER GASBAG

Favorite mugging attack is to pull victim's feet out from under. When victim hits pavement face first he is wrecked. *Bellywhopper Gasbag* prevents this. Balance gauge (A) inflates Belly Bag when victim tilts 45 degrees. This not only cushions fall but also forces noxious gas out rear vent right into attacker's face.

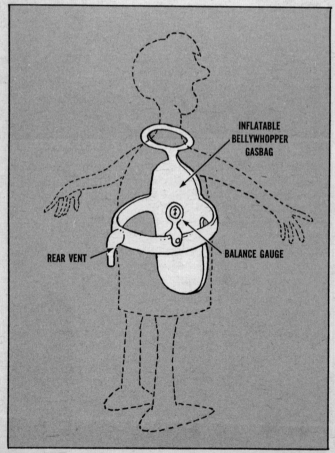

INFLATABLE
BELLYWHOPPER
GASBAG

REAR VENT

BALANCE GAUGE

GACK

PICKPOCKET-PROOF WALLET

This simple but effective device foils pickpockets. Real wallet slips inside phony casing. Strong string or chain attached to wallet has powerful clip that attaches to the inside of pocket. When pickpocket grabs "wallet" all he winds up with is cheap plastic casing.

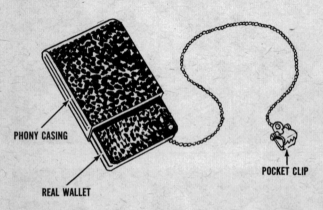

PHONY CASING

REAL WALLET

POCKET CLIP

MECHANIZED TRAP DRAWERS

Drawers with time delay mechanisms are set before retiring, or when leaving house. When burglar opens drawer it allows him two seconds to reach in and then slams shut with tremendous force. Burglar's hands are sometimes chopped off.

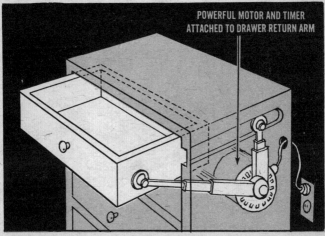

POWERFUL MOTOR AND TIMER
ATTACHED TO DRAWER RETURN ARM

KA CHOONG

WINDOW GRIP

Favorite entrance way of most burglars is window. When burglar enters window shown here and steps on window sill treadle, yoke-like gripping devices spring out and hold him tight. Fat burglars are in particular trouble.

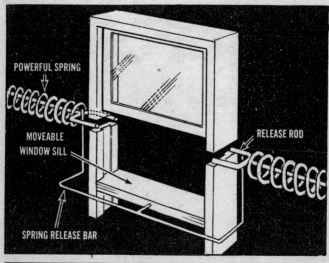

POWERFUL SPRING

MOVEABLE WINDOW SILL

RELEASE ROD

SPRING RELEASE BAR

BLINDING FIREWORKS HAT

Concealed within hat are series of flares. Any blow or pressure on "victim's" head or shoulders releases blinding flares. Victim escapes unaffected because of special dark glasses. Attacker suffers glare blindness for days afterwards — time enough for police to find him.

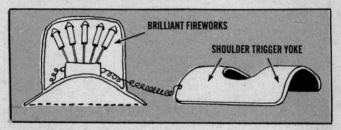

BRILLIANT FIREWORKS

SHOULDER TRIGGER YOKE

HIGHLY CHARGED COAT

Coat is made with copper wires woven into its design. 1,000 replacable penlite batteries are concealed inside. Rubber lining protects wearer, but unsuspecting attacker is nearly executed when he attacks with bare hands.

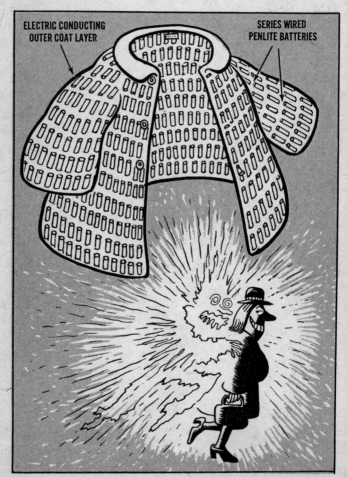

ELECTRIC CONDUCTING
OUTER COAT LAYER

SERIES WIRED
PENLITE BATTERIES

PERSONAL REAR VIEW MIRROR

As noted before, most attackers count on surprise and pounce from behind. Personal rear view mirrors for all occasions would cut this crime problem down to size.

PHONY DOG SHADOW

Guard dogs are extremely effective burglar discouragers. Unfortunately, they are expensive, need care and can eat you out of house and home. This simple device is effective substitute.

ELECTRIC
MOTOR CAUSES
LIFELIKE
MOVEMENT

Section 2. Parking Problems

There are thousands of good parking spaces in a big city. There are also thousands of good reasons why you can't use them. Some are reserved for fire hydrants, driveways, and loading zones. Others are reserved for diplomats, doctors, and doctors' wives in town shopping. The rest are filled with abandoned cars. There's only one solution left. Devices that open up spaces for you and me.

PHONY PARKING METER CAP

Phony parking meter cap fits over regular parking meter. Phony cap contains a battery driven timer that resets itself and never allows time to run out. Car can be parked forever free.

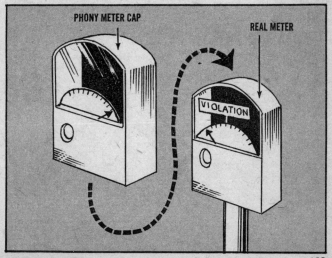

PHONY METER CAP

REAL METER

VIOLATION

PHONY WASTEBASKET AND DUMMY HYDRANT

Collapsible city-type wastebasket (complete with waste) fits in trunk of car. When car is parked next to fire hydrant, wastebasket is placed over it. Dummy hydrant is now placed a space away so cop won't wonder where it went.

REAL HYDRANT

PHONY WASTEBASKET

PHONY HYDRANT

PHONY PARKING SIGN

Inexpensive and easy to use. Sign changes "PARK-ING PROHIBITED" to "PARKING PER-MITTED". Made of thin, magnetized metal, it is lifted into position on top of regular metal sign with special long tongs. Passing cop thinks regulations have been changed. Of course, when you leave you remove it so space will be available next time you need it.

REMOVABLE YELLOW PLASTIC CURB PAINT

Special feature of this plastic paint is it dries instantly, looks permanent, and peels off easily. In the morning when you step out of your apartment and go to your car, you quickly paint the curb yellow and drive away. When you reach the yellow "marked" parking space in front of your office, you park and quickly strip off the yellow film. At night you return to the "yellow space" at home. And so on. Naturally, a certain amount of secrecy is essential.

DRIVES DOWNTOWN TO PREVIOUSLY PREPARED "YELLOW" SPACE IN FRONT OF OFFICE...

PARKS, PEELS UP DRIED YELLOW PLASTIC PAINT...

GOES INTO OFFICE SECURE IN KNOWLEDGE CAR IS SAFE AND ALSO THAT "YELLOW" SPACE AWAITS HIM ON RETURN HOME.

Section 3. Doggie-Do Problems

Cities are terrible places for dogs. City sidewalks are even worse places for dog byproducts. But since you can't outlaw dogs, the next best thing is to keep the streets clean. These inventions do that. (Editor's note: In the interest of good taste we are not going to demonstrate these devices with real dog-do. What we will show are actually plastic replicas. If you see anything else that's your disgusting problem.)

SINGLE ACTION SCOOP

One squeeze of the handle brings brush forward sweeping the offending matter into the scoop for proper disposal.

VACUUM CANE PICKUP

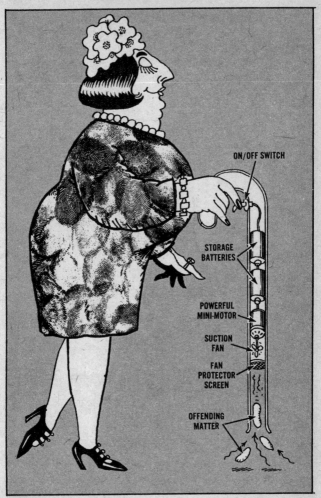

Open end of cane is placed over offending matter. "On" switch causes powerful suction fan to suck matter up in cane. "Off" switch releases suction for convenient, clean, easy disposal of offending matter.

USED CAN PICKUP

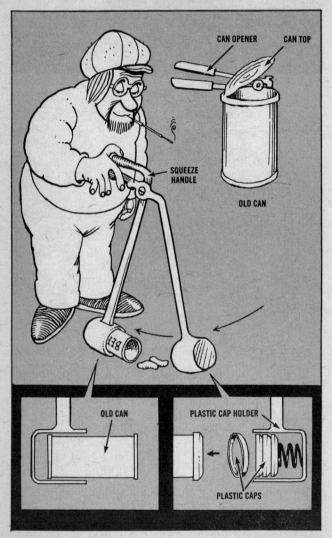

CAN OPENER

CAN TOP

SQUEEZE HANDLE

OLD CAN

OLD CAN

PLASTIC CAP HOLDER

PLASTIC CAPS

A double duty device. It not only gets rid of offending dog matter, but it also helps rid our streets of unsightly old beer and soda cans.

HANDBAG PACKAGING UNIT

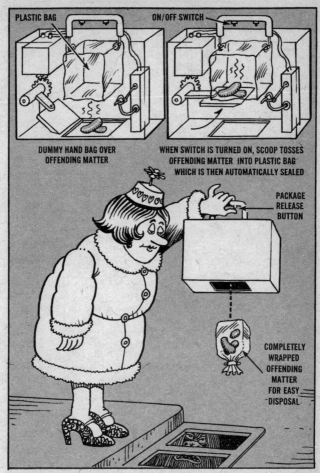

PLASTIC BAG

ON/OFF SWITCH

DUMMY HAND BAG OVER
OFFENDING MATTER

WHEN SWITCH IS TURNED ON, SCOOP TOSSES
OFFENDING MATTER INTO PLASTIC BAG
WHICH IS THEN AUTOMATICALLY SEALED

PACKAGE
RELEASE
BUTTON

COMPLETELY
WRAPPED
OFFENDING
MATTER
FOR EASY
DISPOSAL

Some people are easily embarrassed and for them
this type of dummy bag (or attaché case) is perfect.
When spotting offending matter, all that needs doing
is to put the bag over it and the rest is easy as pie.
Inside a completely automated packaging unit takes
over and in eight seconds a completely wrapped
plastic package pops out for easy disposal.

CENTRIFUGAL POOP CATCHER

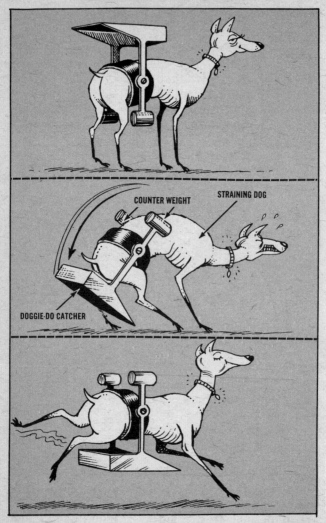

As dog strains and bends backwards, weight shifts and poop catcher swings down to catch and hold dog's offering. When dog stands erect, weight of doggie-do holds container down until it's emptied.

CHEMICAL "WARNING" ELEMENTS IN DOG FOOD

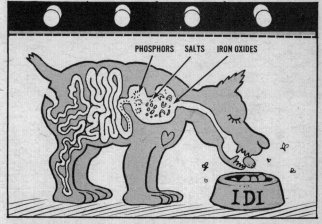

A law should require dog food manufacturers to put a certain chemical compound into their products. It would be composed of harmless phosphors, salts and iron oxides. These elements would enter the dog's digestive system and then turn up in his daily deposits. The following benefits would accrue.

CHEMICAL "WARNING" ELEMENTS IN DOG FOOD

a Phosphors would cause offending matter to glow in the dark to protect night strollers.

b Salts, similar in effect to snow melting salts, would eliminate winter "poopy traps" by revealing light snow covering.

c Iron oxides would be magnetized to set off *beeper* alarms carried by approaching blind persons.

Chapter Nine

Pollution has become a world problem. More and more, government has become concerned with this serious health hazard. But just cleaning up rivers, automobiles, and bad breath isn't enough. There is an even more terrible form of pollution that all of us face every day. *Smokers*. Not only is their tobacco smoke utterly disgusting to the non-smoker, but it is also harmful to the smoker himself. Now, since the government has no compunction whatsoever about controlling dangerous substances like marijuana, drugs, auto emissions, liquor and hair sprays — there is no reason it can't effectively regulate tobacco smoke. This can be done simply by requiring smokers to use . . .

DEVICES THAT STOP SMOKING POLLUTION

COMPLETELY ENCLOSED, NON-POLLUTING PIPE, HOLDERS CIGARETTE, AND CIGAR

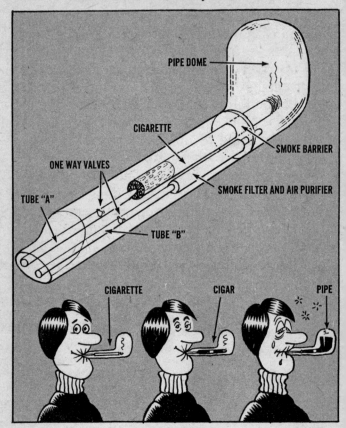

HOW IT WORKS

Smoke is inhaled through "A" tube. Smoker exhales into "B" tube. Filter in "B" removes harmful ingredients. Clean air then goes to enclosed smoke dome, ready to be inhaled into tobacco bowl for return trip to mouth. Completely enclosed system never allows filthy smoke to reach innocent bystanders.

SMOKE FILLED PLASTIC BALLOON SYSTEM

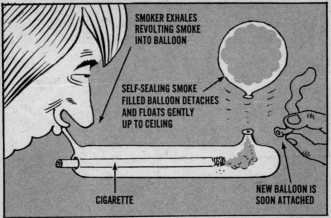

SMOKER EXHALES
REVOLTING SMOKE
INTO BALLOON

SELF-SEALING SMOKE
FILLED BALLOON DETACHES
AND FLOATS GENTLY
UP TO CEILING

CIGARETTE

NEW BALLOON IS
SOON ATTACHED

No longer do crowded rooms need to be filled with smoke. With this simple, fun-to-use device, smoke is safely blown into plastic balloons that float harmlessly to the ceiling for later gathering and disposal. They even add a delightfully provoking decorative touch.

INDIVIDUAL AND MULTIPLE TOBACCO SMOKE
EXHAUSTING DEVICES

Suspended head domes with pull cords are easily
lowered by smokers as shown. Powerful exhaust
fan filters and harmlessly blows air outdoors.

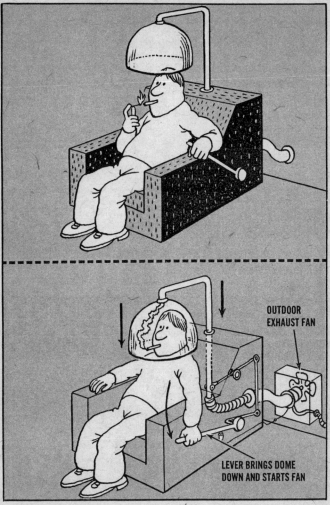

OUTDOOR
EXHAUST FAN

LEVER BRINGS DOME
DOWN AND STARTS FAN

Chair back head dome and exhaust operates simply by pushing lever. Smoke is thus safely exhausted outside. Longer flexible hoses can be attached to increase chair's mobility.

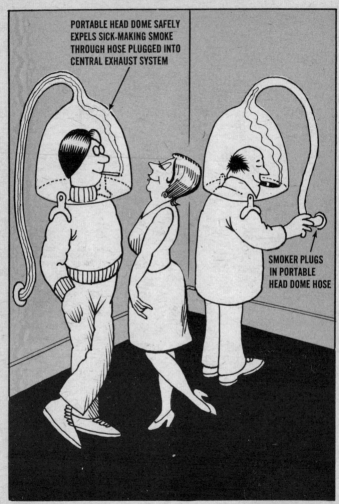

Portable plug-in head dome can be carried around room and plugged into conveniently located exhaust outlets. Good for tightly packed places such as theatres, stadiums, etc.

PERSONAL MASK AND ATTACHE CASE SMOKE FILTER

SMOKING SCARF WITH SELF-CONTAINED PURIFYING FILTER

EFFICIENT NECK YOKE SMOKE FILTER

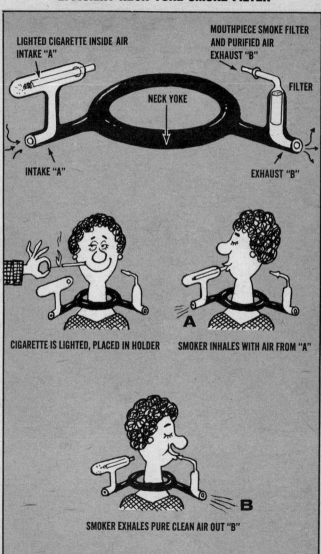

LIGHTED CIGARETTE INSIDE AIR INTAKE "A"

MOUTHPIECE SMOKE FILTER AND PURIFIED AIR EXHAUST "B"

FILTER

NECK YOKE

INTAKE "A"

EXHAUST "B"

CIGARETTE IS LIGHTED, PLACED IN HOLDER

SMOKER INHALES WITH AIR FROM "A"

A

SMOKER EXHALES PURE CLEAN AIR OUT "B"

B

WINDOW CLIP SMOKE EXHAUST DEVICE

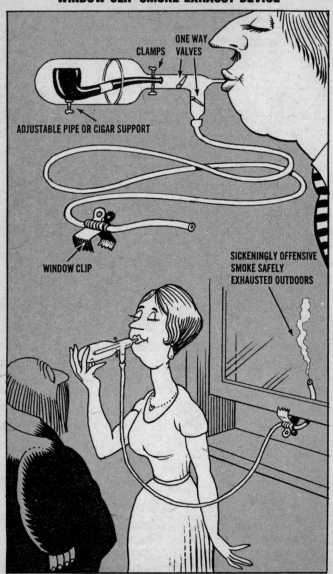

Chapter Ten

HERE WE GO AGAIN WITH. . .

MORE

BUILT-IN OBSOLESCENCE

HIDDEN KEY FILER

KEY   KEYHOLE   HIDDEN KEY FILE

Lock has small hidden file that wears down key. Filings also jam lock for early replacement.

TOP POPPER ON FELT-TIPPED MARKER

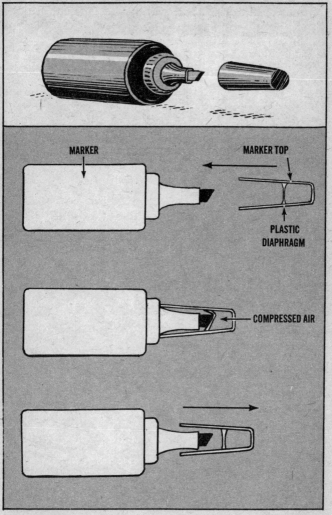

MARKER

MARKER TOP

PLASTIC DIAPHRAGM

COMPRESSED AIR

Top is designed to compress and trap air. After a while pressure builds up and pops top loose just enough to dry up fluid.

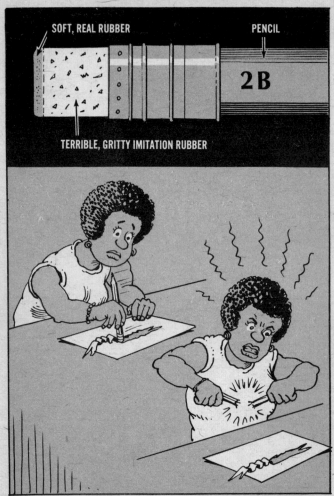

SOFT, REAL RUBBER

PENCIL

2 B

TERRIBLE, GRITTY IMITATION RUBBER

Eraser tip on pencil is made of two kinds of rubber. Top sixteenth of an inch is wonderful soft rubber. After that, it's a paper tearing, gritty piece of junk. User either has to buy an eraser or a whole new pencil.

ITCHY SOAP

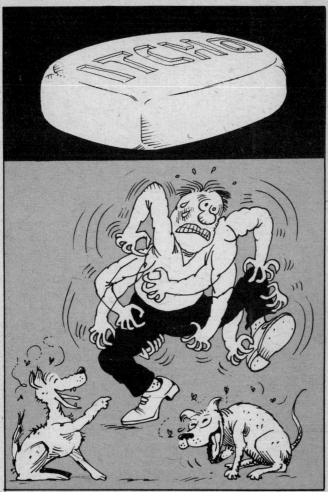

This soap deposits a water resistant layer of invisible chemical film on bather's body. After about six hours chemical causes itching which makes person think he needs another bath or shower. Soap gets used up more quickly and user never suspects why.

BUTTON LOSERS

Centers of buttons are scored in such a way as to snap out after some use. User thinks broken thread caused button's loss.

LEAKY BALL POINT PENS

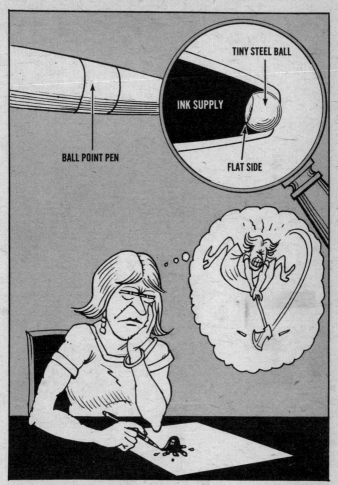

TINY STEEL BALL

INK SUPPLY

BALL POINT PEN

FLAT SIDE

This tiny, almost invisible ball in tip of ball point pen is made so it is not exactly round. When it rolls on paper and reaches flat spot a big blob of ink spurts out. This not only uses up ink faster but may cause disgusted user to discard whole pen.

SOFT METAL SPOTS

THE SHORTEST
DISTANCE BETWEEN
TWO POINTS IS
A STRAIGHT LINE.
EXAMPLE:

A   B

Ruler's metal edge is made with soft spots that soon wear out causing wavy lines. Ruler becomes virtually useless.

TOOTHPASTE TUBE AIR POCKET

Back end of tube is filled with air. As toothpaste is used, air moves to front and when it's released consumer thinks toothpaste is used up.

Paint goes on fine first time. But when another coat is put on in future, first coat slowly bleeds through. User puts on coat after coat. Bleed through stops after six or seven coats, but a lot of paint is used up.

Chapter Eleven

Every day we use things that are created without regard to the problems that might crop up when they are actually in use. For example, when the automobile was invented no one gave a single thought to parking problems. Today that's a driver's biggest nightmare. On the following pages you will find solutions to such problems with . . .

INVENTIONS THAT MAKE OTHER INVENTIONS WORK BETTER

INVENTION: Digital Watch

PROBLEM:

Third hand sometimes needed to press button.

SOLUTION:

Mechanical third hand attaches with simple harness. It is controlled by various shoulder movements and about 3 to 4 months of practice will normally achieve proficiency.

INVENTION: Mini Calculator

PROBLEM:

Keys too small for fingers.

SOLUTION:

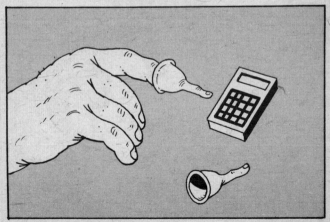

"Fony Fingers" plastic finger tips with tiny plastic fingers. Also useful for spearing olives, back scratching, and picking teeth.

INVENTION: Hair Sprays

PROBLEM:

Entire face gets poisonous chemicals.

SOLUTION:

Personalized plastic head masks with breathing tube. Only hair is exposed to deadly sprays.

INVENTION: Automatic Toll Collector

PROBLEM:

Opening window in cold, rain or snow.

SOLUTION:

Coin gun is loaded with coins of all denominations.
Key punch sets amount and the pressed trigger de-
livers it unerringly into basket. Caution: Don't use it
when there's a human toll collector. Serious injury
could occur.

INVENTION: Modern Urinals

PROBLEM:

Public pigs toss cigarettes, cigars, matchbooks and other garbage to clog and to create disgusting removal problems.

SOLUTION:

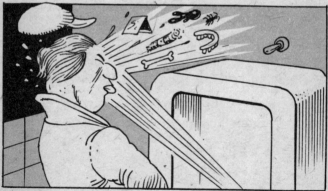

Special pitching devices in bottom of urinal remains inactive as long as liquid is hitting it. But moment liquid stops, it starts pitching out any solid objects thrown in. Careless user does not soon forget this lesson.

INVENTION: Earphone Type Portable Radio

PROBLEM:

Blocks out all other sound.

SOLUTION:

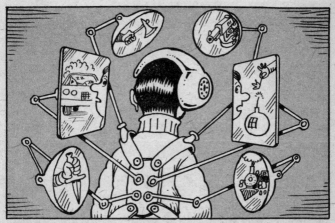

Series of rear view mirrors on shoulder harness lets you see dangers such as oncoming vehicles, holdup men, bomb throwers, etc. all around you.

INVENTION: Auto Antenna

PROBLEM:

Broken off by vandals.

SOLUTION:

Antenna is electrified and freezes vandal's hand until police arrive.

INVENTION: Automatic Drinking Fountain

PROBLEM:

People with diseases may put mouths (yecch!) on fountain head.

SOLUTION:

Fountain head guard triggers device that shoots out and hits nose of person whose mouth gets too close to fountain head. Though no permanent damage is done, drinker is somewhat more cautious.

INVENTION: Multi-Channel Sound Systems

PROBLEM:

To find best listening spot in any room.

SOLUTION:

Triangulation beeper is carried by listener. When perfect spot is reached, beeper signals. Listener stops right on that spot, secure in knowledge he's getting perfect multi-channel reception.

144

INVENTION: Public Toilets

PROBLEM:

Unsanitary condition of public toilets.

SOLUTION:

Revolving toilets rotate after use. When patron departs, closing door sets toilet in motion and it goes into disinfecting chamber for complete cleaning and sanitizing service.

INVENTION: Streamlined Cars

PROBLEM:

Low slung cars do not allow driver to see anything except rear bumper of the car ahead.

SOLUTION:

Add-on accordion plastic bubble. Car keeps racy low shape. But when there's trouble ahead and you're stuck in traffic, standing up to look and see is now possible. Also good on long trips for stretching legs once in a while.

Chapter Twelve

We all love and depend on the marvelous creations that inventive geniuses have produced to make our lives pleasanter and easier. But like everything else in this world, they're not always perfect. When you relax and rely on them, and they let you down, then you're much worse off than you would have been without them. For some major offenders in this category, here is . . .

THE INVENTIONS HATE BOOK

DON'T YOU HATE . . .

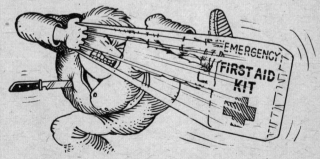

Plastic wrappings that are near impossible to break through.

Beverage can tabs that snap off without opening the can.

DON'T YOU HATE . . .

Electric can openers that skip and ruin the lip for other openers.

Swivel wheels on carts and furniture that never go in the direction you want to go.

DON'T YOU HATE . . .

Parking meters whose coin-taking mechanism works when the rest of it is out of order.

Glorious, full-color package photos that the inside product cannot hope to match.

DON'T YOU HATE . . .

Built-in calculator batteries that go dead and can't be replaced.

DON'T YOU HATE . . .

No-leak batteries that corrode inside valuable equipment.

DON'T YOU HATE . . .

Toothbrush bristles that come out and stick in your gums.

Paper rolls that tear the wrong way.

Ball point pens that become un-retracted.

DON'T YOU HATE . . .

Exact change toll baskets that fail to register your deposit.

DON'T YOU HATE . . .

Toasters with a dozen settings that can't turn out what you want!

DON'T YOU HATE . . .

Vending machines with faulty coin return buttons.

DON'T YOU HATE . . .

Sophisticated direct dialing telephone systems that get wrong long-distance numbers.

DON'T YOU HATE . . .

Cheap synthetic fabrics that have to be treated with more care than the finest silks.

DON'T YOU HATE . . .

Handkerchiefs and towels made of plastic fibers that have no absorption power whatsoever.

Having to prove a computer made the mistake, not you.

Multi-layered sales receipts that leave no impression on the copy you need for credit or exchange.

Chapter Thirteen

When the Arabs gave us the business on oil, they affected every facet of our lives. Some of the pressure is already upon us in higher costs. But the worst is yet to come, and the full impact won't be felt for years. One area where we will all soon feel the pinch has to do with living space. Large spaces are not only costlier to build, but heating and air-conditioning them becomes prohibitively expensive. Private home and apartment dwellers will be particularly affected. They will be getting less and less space for their money. So with this in mind, here are suggestions for . . .

SMALLER LIVING SPACES MADE TO LOOK BIG AND COMFORTABLE

These have often been used to give the effect of more space. Of course, while they're reflecting more space they are also reflecting more people in the space. This may give you a feeling of crowding. However, if you are bothered by loneliness, it could help take the feeling away.

PHONY DOORS AND WINDOWS

These are simple, inexpensive molded plastic paste-ons that give the illusion of more rooms and open areas. They come in shapes and styles to suit every need.

PLAIN DOOR

It is pasted on wall simply to give the effect that there's another room in the dwelling. Especially effective in one room apartments.

This door creates a feeling of space by revealing an outdoor view that fits in with the neighborhood. Not recommended in cities with high crime rates as a nervous breakdown can ensue.

Like Dutch doors, window can open onto favored scene. Also available with sliding sash so it can be closed and "locked" by those too nervous to sleep with an open window.

PICTURE WINDOWS

These, when placed on wall can turn even tiny, dingy, slum apartments into spacious palaces. Drapery adds a luxurious touch of realism.

PERSPECTIVE WALLPAPER

Many artists are famous for drawing pictures with such realistic perspectives that people say they literally feel they could walk into them. These wallpapers have the same effect. Of course, after a while you will get used to it all and will stop walking *"into"* your walls. But be sure to watch unsuspecting visitors carefully.

This time-honored device has been used for years by home builders. By furnishing their model homes with half-sized furniture, they fooled prospective buyers into thinking they were getting spacious houses. Of course, when their own normal sized furniture arrived on moving day, there wasn't room enough left to stand. But now, this wonderful bit of American know-how can benefit you. Tiny furniture is just what you need to make the tiny living space you have look normal size.

This is another time honored method of creating space. There really is no reason why a room should be cluttered and crowded with items that are not in constant use.

To go a step further than built-ins, we have paste-on molded plastic or paper furniture. A room without furniture is depressing. But a lot of attractive pieces are useless and take up space. These can be produced in flat form with a 3D effect and the room will look cozily furnished with lots of room to move around.

Chapter Fourteen

The world is full of lonely clods who have no relatives, friends or pets. The world is also full of miserable show-offs who won't let lonely clods forget that they don't have any relatives, friends or pets. They rub it in by filling their desks and wallets with pictures showing vast hordes of loved ones. So if you're one of the poor left out slobs, here's your chance to show up those show off creeps. On the following pages you will find a gallery of relatives, friends and pets that you can clip out and frame for your desk or carry in your wallet.

WALLET AND DESK PICTURES FOR LONELY CLODS

Some People show off their wonderful family and friends with big wallet picture displays.

Some people show off their wonderful family and friends with big desk picture displays.

Some people stand around feeling like glitch since they don't have any wonderful family or friends or pictures.

If that's *your* problem, fret no more. Just take your scissors and turn the page.

CUT ALONG DOTTED LINES

Here is a wonderful shot of a kid brother. Just cut along the dotted line and put in wallet or desk picture frame.

CUT ALONG DOTTED LINES

Here is a wonderful shot of a mother and father. They must love each other very much. They're literally inseparable.

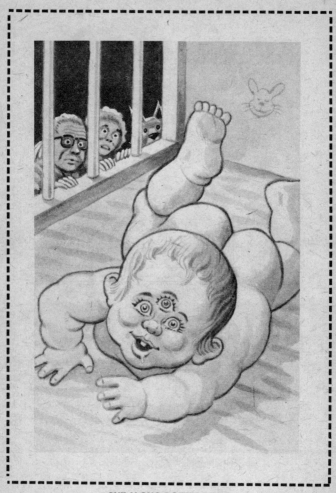

CUT ALONG DOTTED LINES

Here is a wonderful shot of baby. (We said baby. We didn't say baby *what*.)

Here is a wonderful shot of a boy friend. He's small, but oh my.

CUT ALONG DOTTED LINES

Here is a wonderful shot of a girl friend. Won't the fellows down at the office turn green with envy? Well, turn green, anyway.

CUT ALONG DOTTED LINES

Here is a wonderful shot of (a) best friend(s). He (they) is (are) the best friend(s) anyone could ever hope for.

CUT ALONG DOTTED LINES

Here is a wonderful shot of a pet. Isn't it cute and cuddly?

Here's another *terrific inventive idea*.* To easily use the pictures on each side of this page merely purchase a second book.

*A *terrific inventive idea* for doubling book sales!

Chapter Fifteen

Somewhere back in time, when human communication began, someone invented the *sign*. Now it is everywhere — on roads, in stores, in schools, on packages, etc. In fact, life as we know it would come to an immediate standstill if we didn't have signs to tell us where to go, how to dress and what to beware of. Signs come in every shape and form. Some with words — like "stop" and "go" for traffic. Some with pictures — like a skull and crossbones for "poison." Some come with company designs, like Bell Telephone's picture of a bell. As you can see, the person who invented the sign sure started something. But it is work that never ends. The need for new signs is always with us. To satisfy this demand we give you . . .

SIGNS, DESIGNS AND SYMBOL-MINDED FUN

PICTURE ROAD SIGNS

Modern cars travel so fast that it's often impossible to read signs that flash behind before you finish reading. Picture signs solve the problem.

FALLING ROCK ZONE

This simply means that you are playing a sort of Russian road roulette because the highway department figured it was cheaper to put up a sign than to put up a barrier that would prevent the rocks from falling.

BRIBES CHEERFULLY ACCEPTED

Motorists are confused by hinting games played by bribe seeking local officials. Sign in this town, which has been controlled by the same political machine for 124 years, clearly eliminates this confusion.

REST ROOMS

In emergencies this sign is invaluable. At least it gives motorists options, instead of having to go on for miles keeping legs crossed — er — keeping fingers crossed hoping for relief.

ENTERING BUG ZONE

Vicious insects can be a fearsome hazard when highways pass swamps, garbage dumps, and restaurant areas. Sign warns motorist to shut window before attack begins.

FLOOD AREA

This is a serious warning in many areas where inadequate sewers back up and fill roads during slightest drizzle. Signs warn motorist to keep windows open for quick escape.

FOOD AND LODGING AHEAD

Anyone who has turned hopefully off the road seeking food and lodging will appreciate this sign that at least warns you of what you'll find.

FRESH WATER STREAM

City folks think they can stop for a cool drink at any fresh water stream. But many are downstream from deadly chemical plants and the cool drink may leave the drinker colder than a mackerel.

MEAN JUDGE

Driver is advised to be alert, obeying all laws carefully, as this town has a merciless judge.

CONFUSING SIGNS AHEAD

This sign prepares driver to swerve and avoid head-on collision caused by on-coming cars getting into your lane because of confusing signs up ahead.

Picture signs are a great, instantly understood, international language. But even better and quicker to understand are familiar symbols. This is particularly good in business. Since the main interest of business is money, we feel it's a good psychological lift to incorporate the money sign into symbols. Here are some examples of . . .

DOLLAR
IGN
IN
BUSINESS
SYMBOLS

A symbol suggestion for **THE BANK OF AMERICA**

A symbol suggestion for **REMINGTON ARMS**

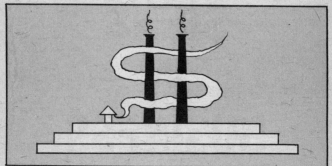

A symbol suggestion for **NATIONAL FOOTBALL LEAGUE**

A symbol suggestion for **NBC TV**

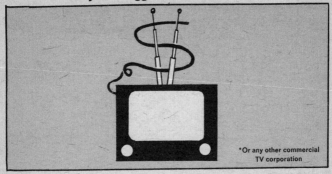

*Or any other commercial
TV corporation

A symbol suggestion for **THE HEART FUND**

A symbol suggestion for **THE U. S. MEDICAL SOCIETY**

A symbol suggestion for
THE DEMOCRATIC PARTY

A symbol suggestion for
THE REPUBLICAN PARTY

A symbol suggestion for **THE UNIFICATION CHURCH**

A symbol suggestion for

For some people word signs work. For others, picture signs work. But for some clods nothing works except to point them in the right direction and hope for the best. And we think the best way is with something like these handy

HAND SIGNS

SURGERY

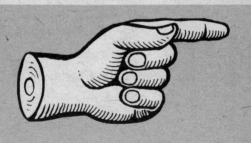

WET PAINT

MARRIAGE BUREAU

GYNECOLOGIST

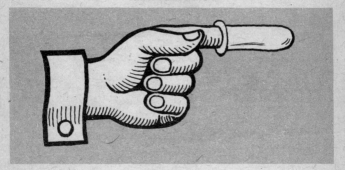

NURSERY

JAIL

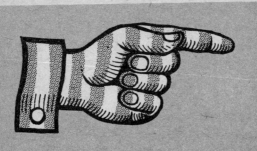

HOT DOG STAND

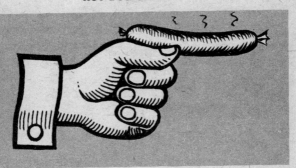

COPYING MACHINE

WATCH DOG

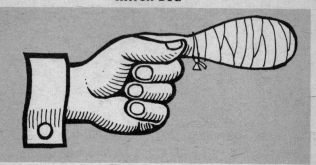

EXPOSED FAN

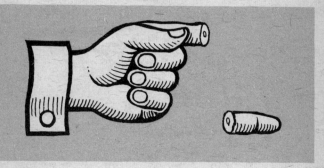

REPAIRS

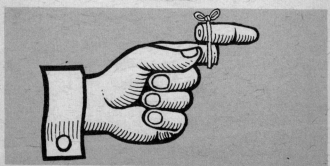

CITY DUMP

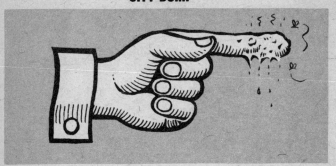

FREAK SHOW

AIRPORT

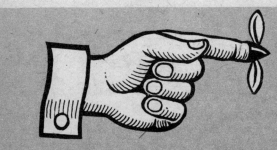

FIRE HOSE

EXPLOSIVES

THE END